STORYLAND

3

Activity Book

Lisiane Ott Schulz

Luciana Santos Pinheiro

Storyland Student's Site Access Code:
Storyland3@students

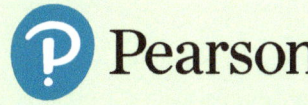

Head of Product - Pearson Brasil	Juliano Costa
Product Manager - Pearson Brasil	Marjorie Robles
Product Coordinator - ELT	Mônica Bicalho
Authors	Lisiane Ott Schulz
	Luciana Santos Pinheiro
Collaborators	Fernanda Bressan Capelini
	Indiana Oliveira
	Milena Schneid Eich
	Sofia Xanthopoulos Bordin
	Verônica Bombassaro
Editor - ELT	Simara H. Dal'Alba
Editorial Assistant - ELT	Sandra Vergani Dall'Agnol
Proofreader	Silva Serviços de Educação
Proofreader (Portuguese):	Fernanda R. Braga Simon
Copyeditor	Maria Estela Alcântara
Teacher's Guide (Portuguese translation)	Eduardo Lubisco Portella
Pedagogical Reviewer	Viviane Kirmeliene
Quality Control	Renata S. C. Victor
Product Design Coordinator	Rafael Lino
Art Editor - ELT	Emily Andrade
Production Editors	Daniel Reis
	Vitor Martins
Acquisitions and permissions Manager	Maiti Salla
Acquisitions and permissions	Sandra Sebastião
Graphic design	Mirella Della Maggiore Armentano
	APIS design integrado
Graphic design (cover)	Daniel Reis
	Emily Andrade
	Mirella Della Maggiore Armentano
Illustration (cover)	Leandro Marcondes
Illustrated by	Alex Cói | Estúdio Secreto
	Bruna Sousa
	Bruno Badain | Manga Mecânica
	Leandro Marcondes
	Marcelo Kina
	Mari Heffner
	Victor Lemos
Content Development	Allya Language Solutions
Media Development	Estação Gráfica
Audio	Maximal Studio

Every effort has been made to trace the copyright holders and we apologize in advance for any unintentional omissions. We would be pleased to insert the appropriate acknowledgement in any subsequent edition of this publication.

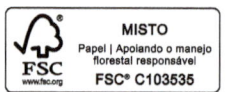

Printed in Brazil by Reproset RPSZ 220713

Dados Internacionais de Catalogação na Publicação (CIP)
(Câmara Brasileira do Livro, SP, Brasil)

Schulz, Lisiane Ott
  Storyland 3: Activity Book / Lisiane Ott Schulz, Luciana Santos Pinheiro; [coordenação Monica Bicalho]. -- 1. ed. -- São Paulo: Pearson Education do Brasil, 2018.

Vários ilustradores.
ISBN 978-85-430-2638-1

1. Inglês (Educação infantil) I. Pinheiro, Luciana Santos. II. Bicalho, Monica. III. Título.

18-17183   CDD-372.21

Índices para catálogo sistemático:
1. Inglês : Educação infantil 372.21
Maria Alice Ferreira - Bibliotecária - CRB-8/7964
ISBN 978-85-430-2638-1 (Activity Book)

STORYLAND

Activity Book 3

UNIT 1	The Lion And The Mouse	4
UNIT 2	Snow White	8
UNIT 3	Aladdin	12
UNIT 4	The Giant Turnip	16
UNIT 5	The Bremen Town Musicians	20
UNIT 6	Little Red Riding Hood	24
UNIT 7	Yankee Doodle	28
UNIT 8	The Princess And The Pea	32

Masks..36

Self-assessment Stickers..................................49

UNIT 1

 **TRACE.**

LESSON 1

2 DRAW.

 LESSON 2

 **MATCH AND COLOR.**

 # 4 CIRCLE.

SELF-ASSESSMENT

LESSON 4

UNIT 2

 COUNT AND CHECK.

 LESSON 1

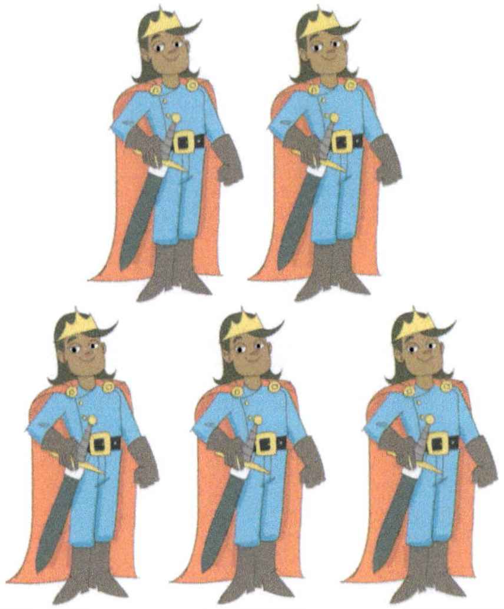

| 4 | 3 | 5 |  | 2 | 4 | 6 |  | 1 | 3 | 5 |
| 2 | 6 | 7 |  | 4 | 2 | 6 |  | 7 | 4 | 3 |

 CIRCLE.

LESSON 2

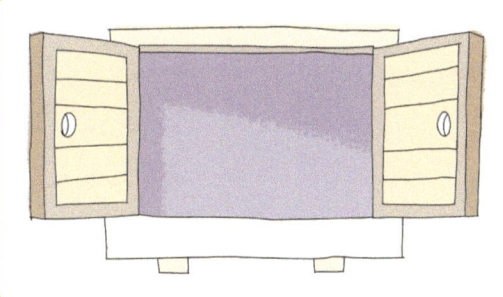  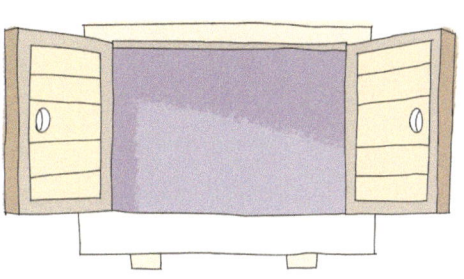 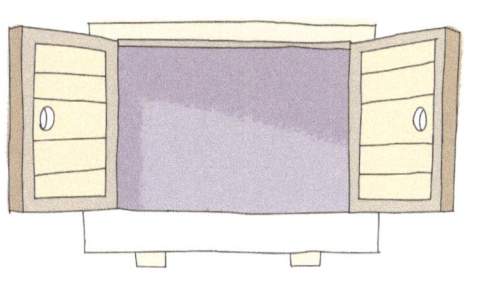

 **LOOK AND COLOR.**

4 PLAY AND SAY.     SELF-ASSESSMENT   LESSON 4

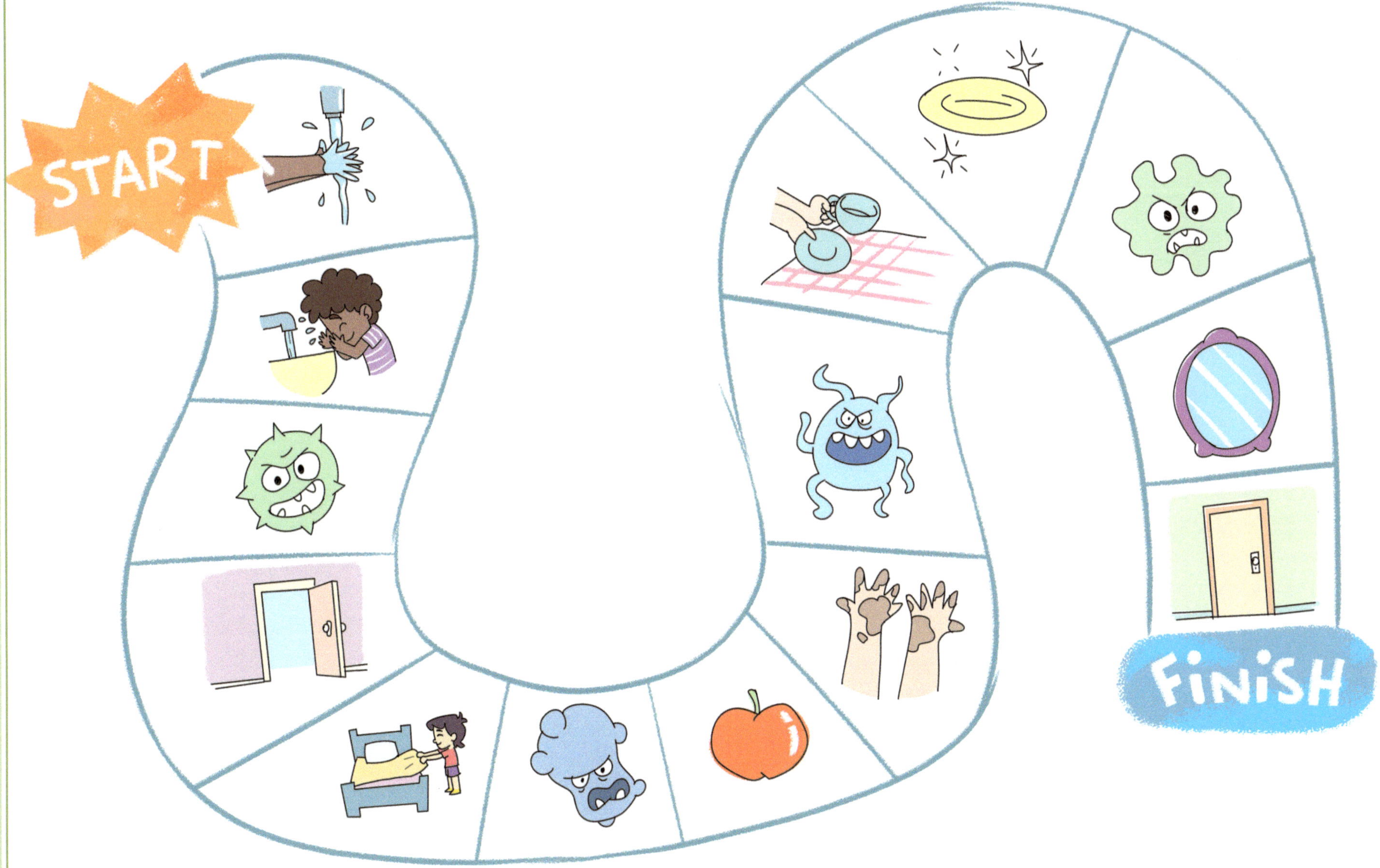

UNIT 3

 COLOR AND SAY.

 LESSON 1

 DRAW AND COLOR.

LESSON 2

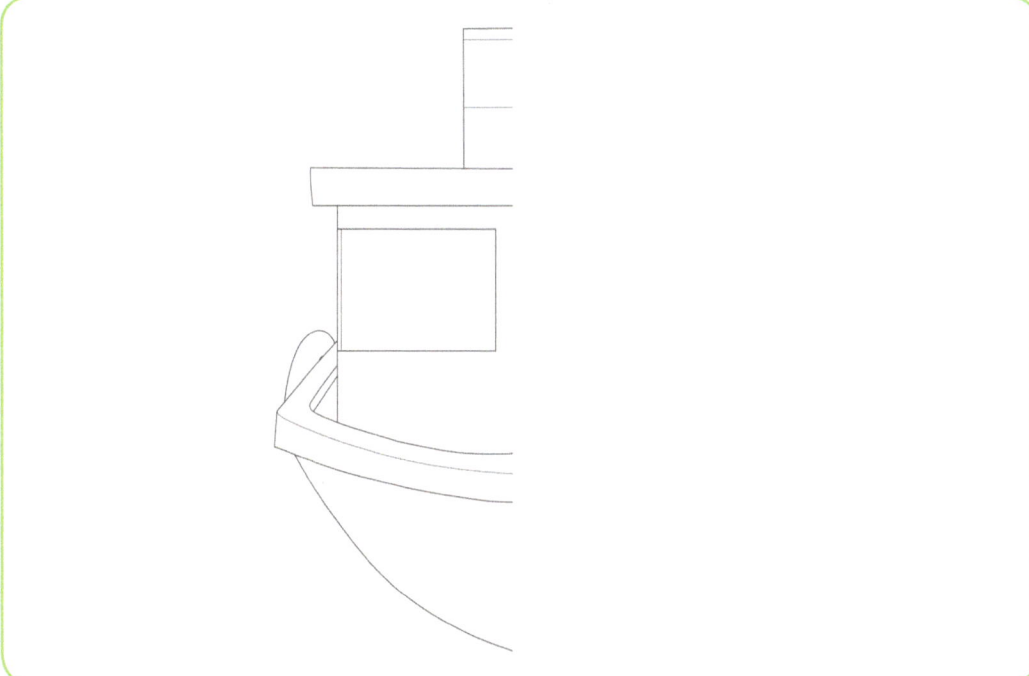
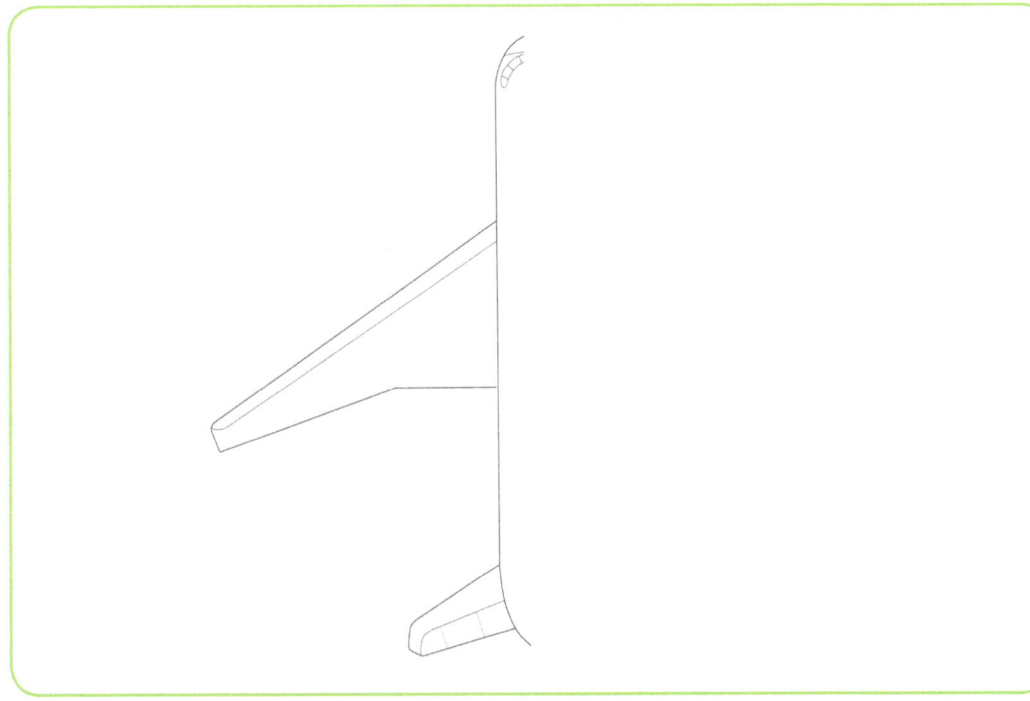

 COLOR.

LESSON 3

4 COUNT AND WRITE.  SELF-ASSESSMENT   LESSON 4

UNIT 4

COUNT AND TRACE.

LESSON 1

SIX

SEVEN

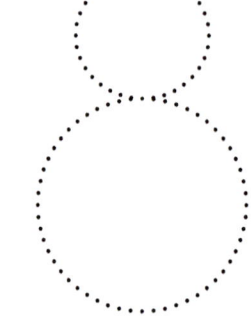
EIGHT

16

2 CIRCLE.

LESSON 2

17

 **DRAW AND COLOR.**

4 COUNT AND COLOR.

SELF-ASSESSMENT

LESSON 4

6	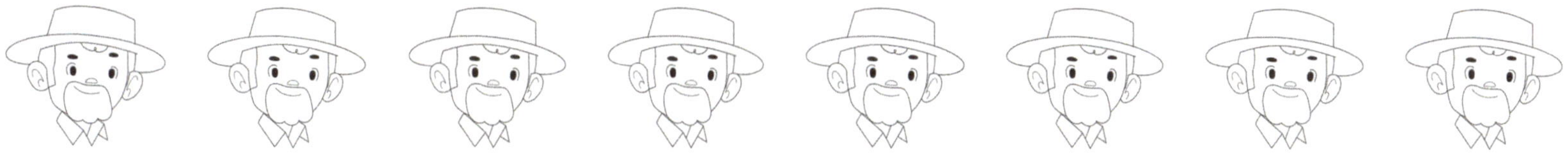
8	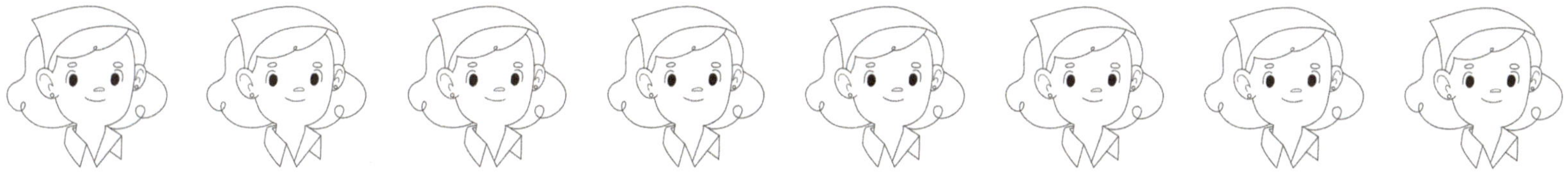
5	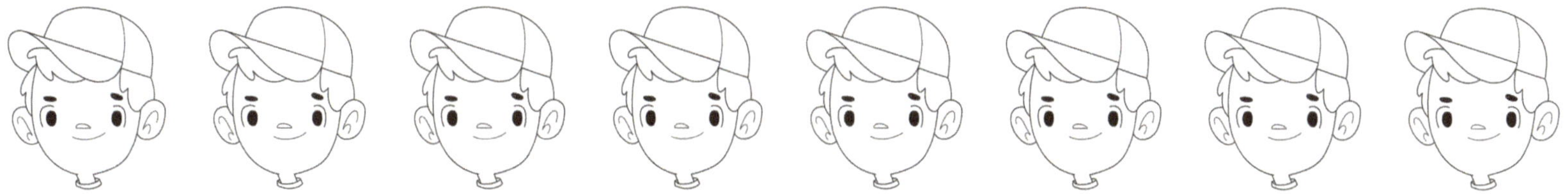
7	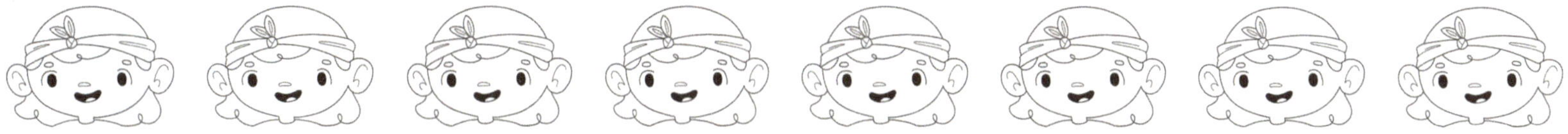
4	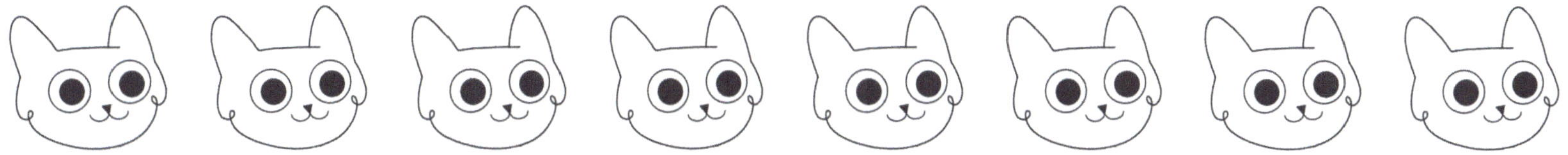

UNIT 5

LOOK AND COLOR.

LESSON 1

 LOOK AND MATCH.

 COUNT AND SAY. THEN DRAW.

4 LOOK, MATCH, AND DRAW.

SELF-ASSESSMENT

LESSON 4

 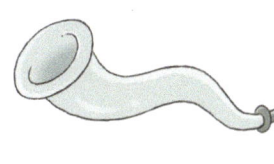   

23

UNIT 6

LOOK AND MATCH.

LESSON 1

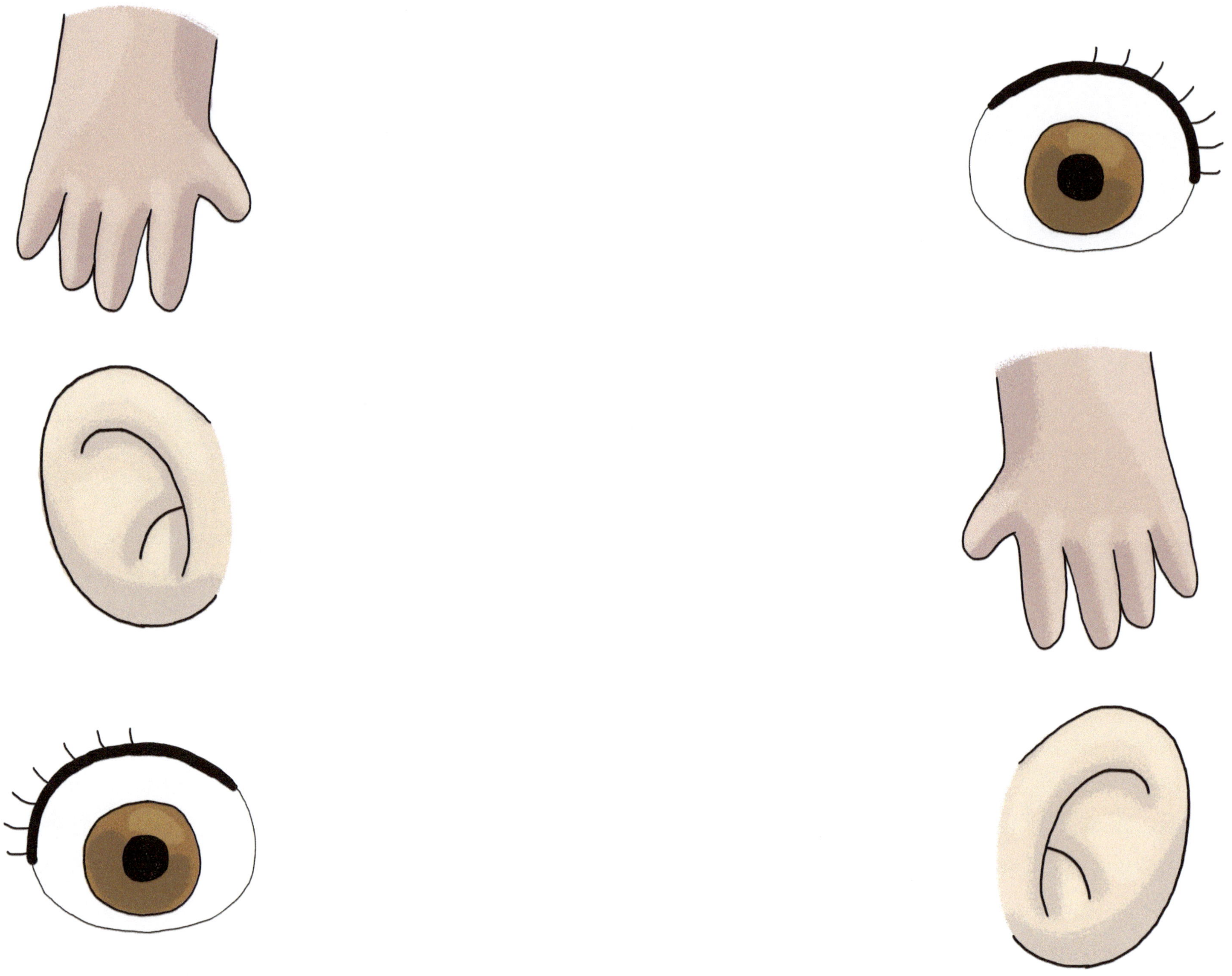

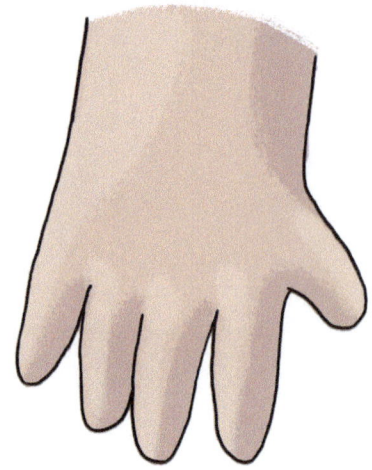
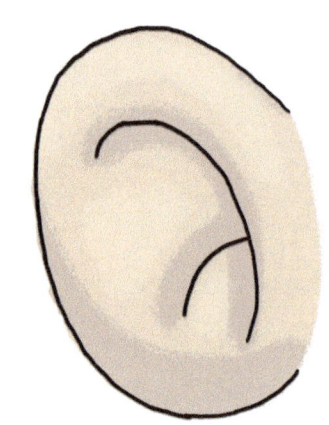
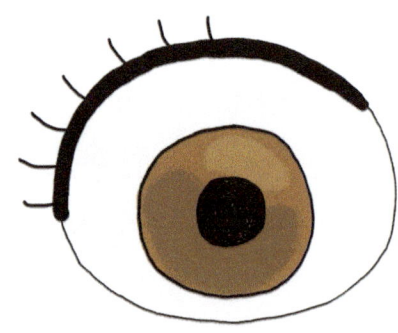
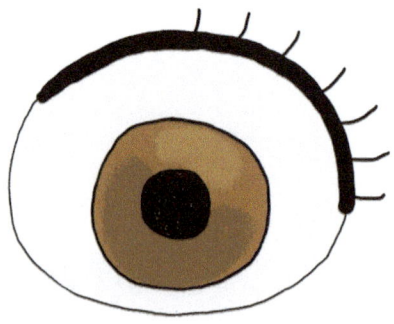
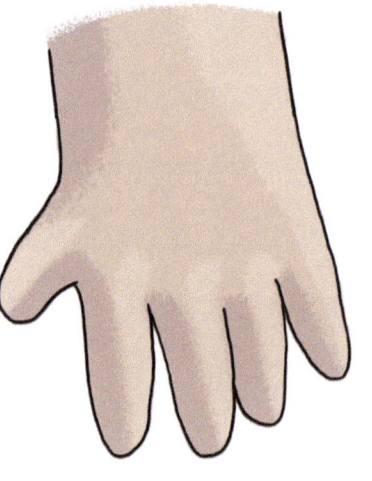
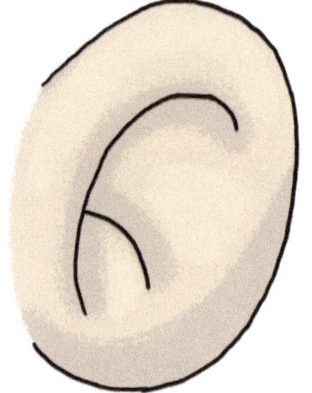

 COUNT AND WRITE.

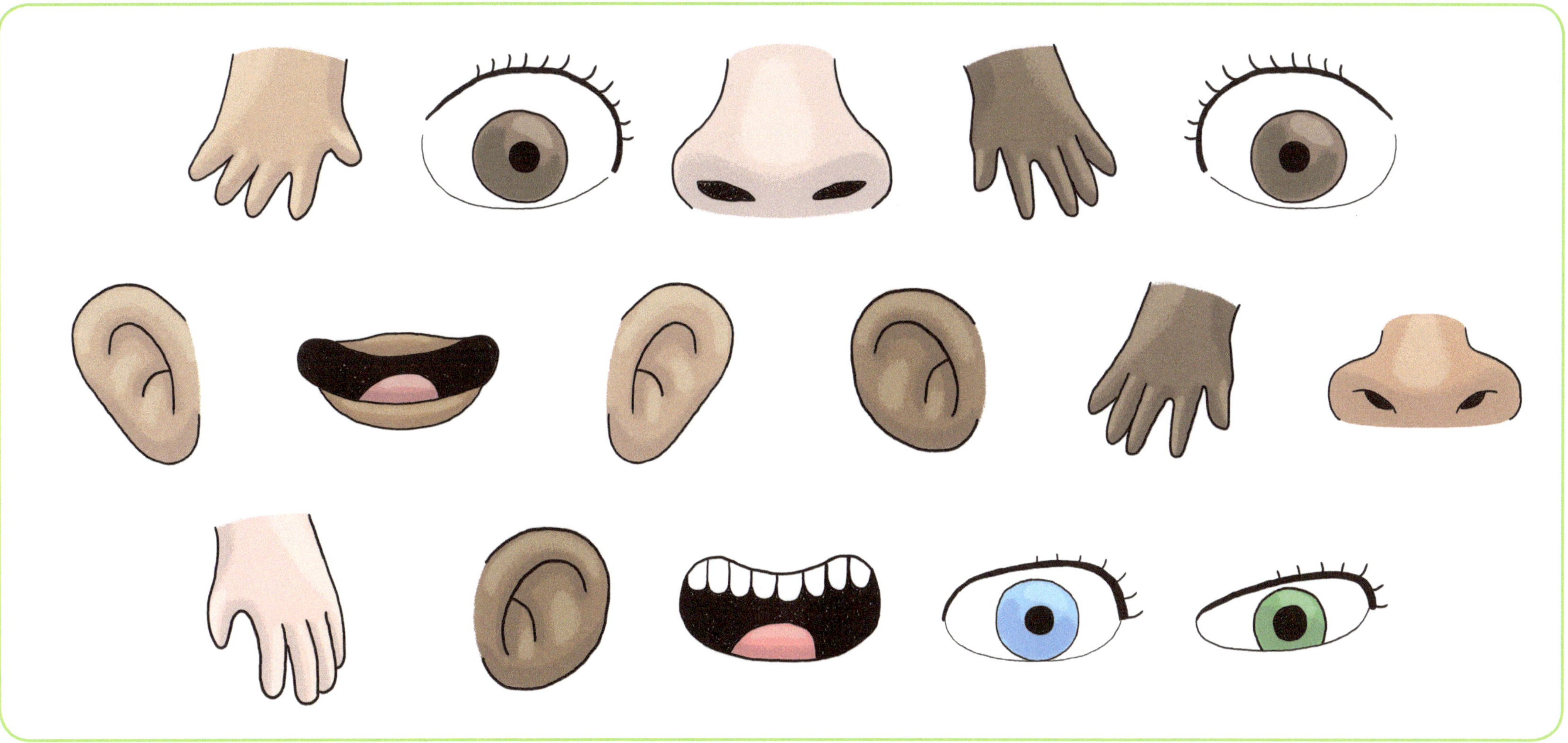

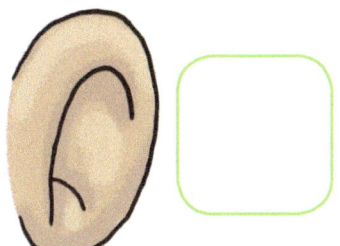   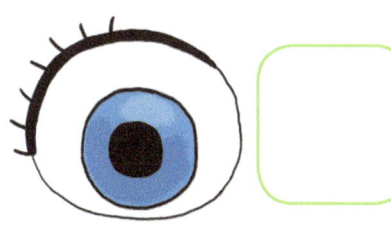

 **MATCH AND COLOR.**

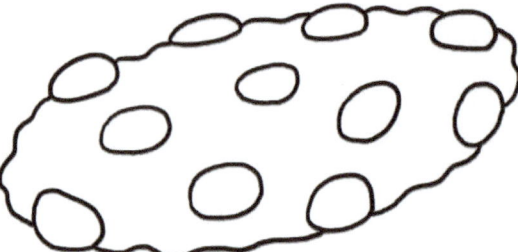

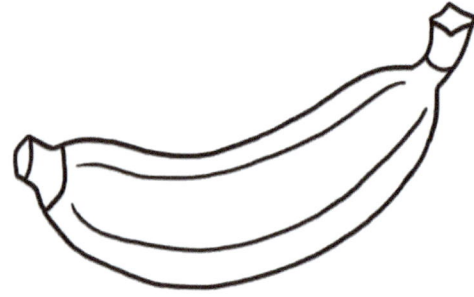
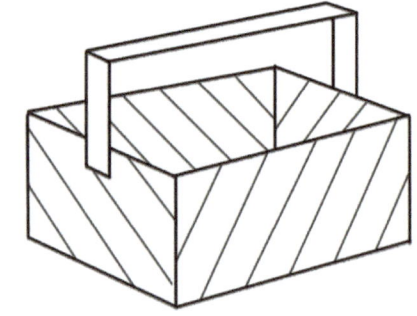

4 CIRCLE.  SELF-ASSESSMENT  LESSON 4

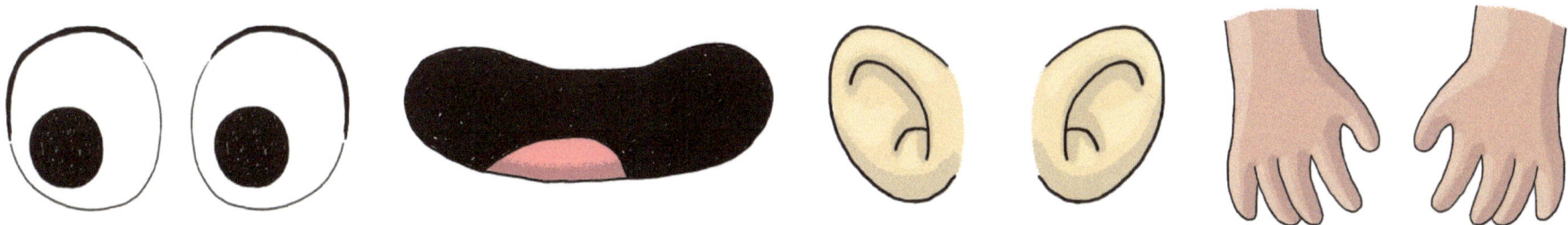

SELF-ASSESSMENT STICKER PAGE 49

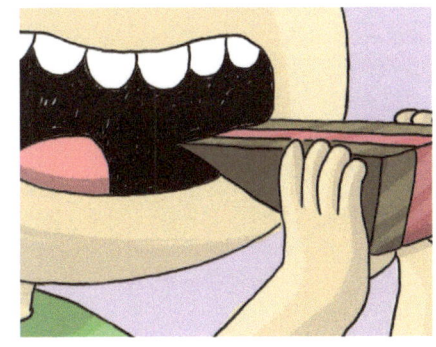 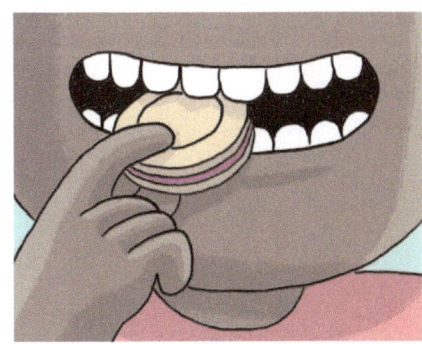  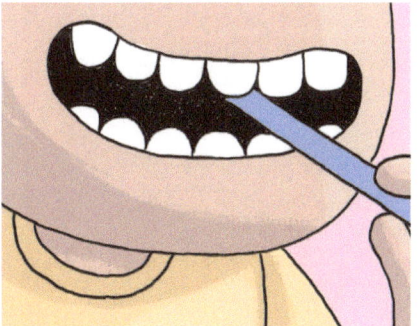

UNIT 7

1 LOOK, SAY, AND COLOR.

LESSON 1

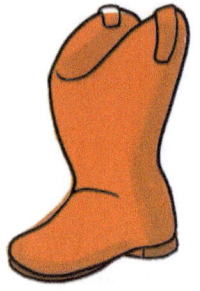 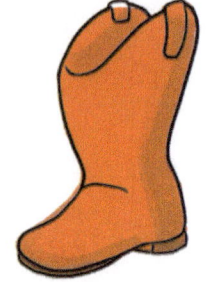 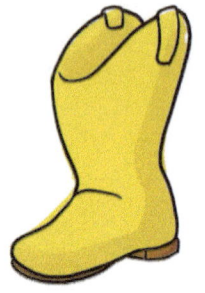 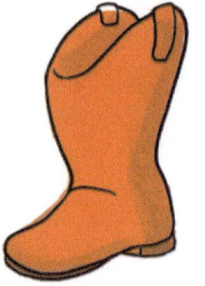 

 LOOK AND MATCH. THEN COLOR.

LESSON 2

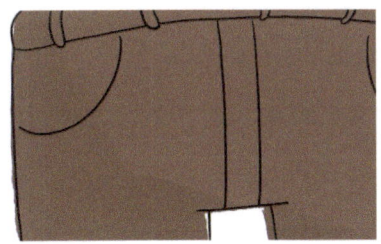  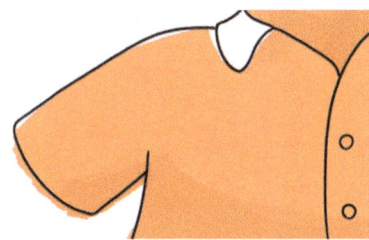  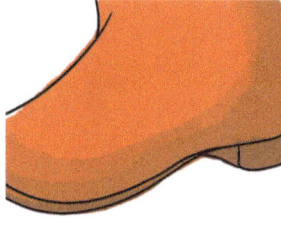

  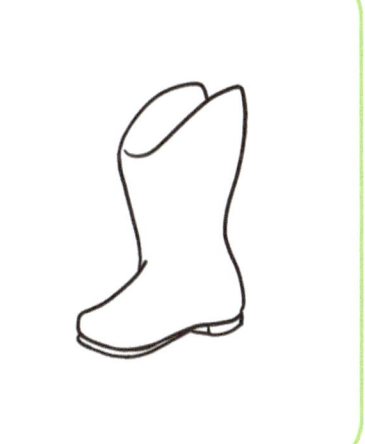  

 LOOK AND MATCH.

| 1-2 | 3-4 | 5-6 | 7-8 | 9-10 |

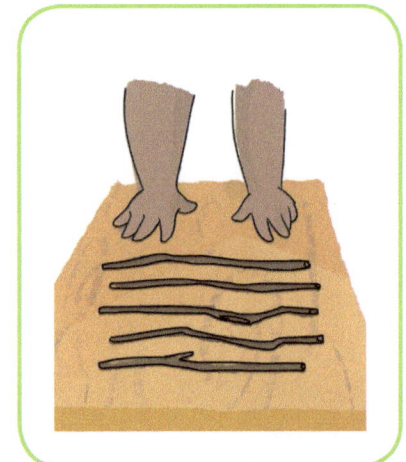    

 COUNT, MATCH, AND COLOR.

SELF-ASSESSMENT

LESSON 4

1 2 3 4 5 6 7 8 9 10

    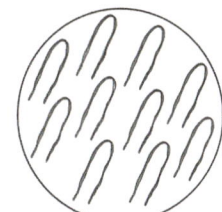

  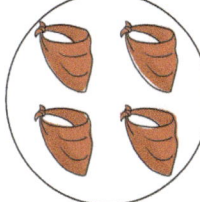 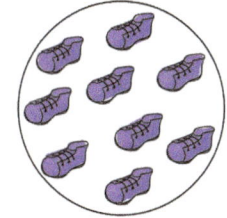 

# COUNT AND MATCH.

LESSON 1

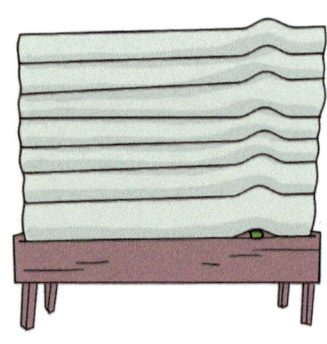 + 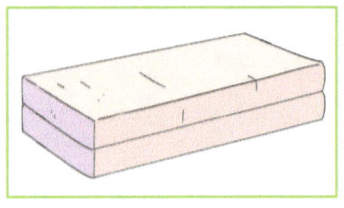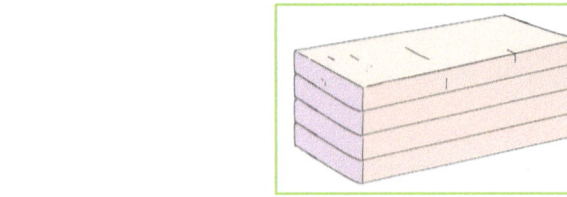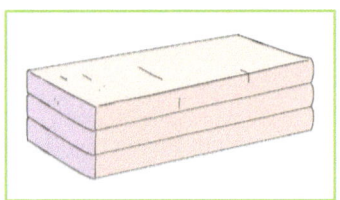 = 10

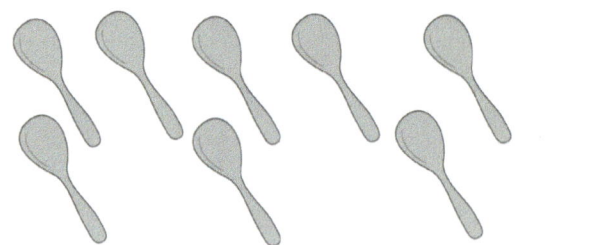 +  = 10

2 DRAW AND SAY.

3 POINT AND CIRCLE.

 COUNT AND COLOR.     SELF-ASSESSMENT

3

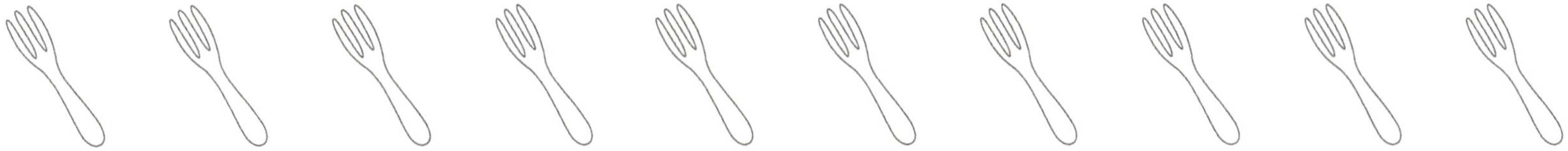

5

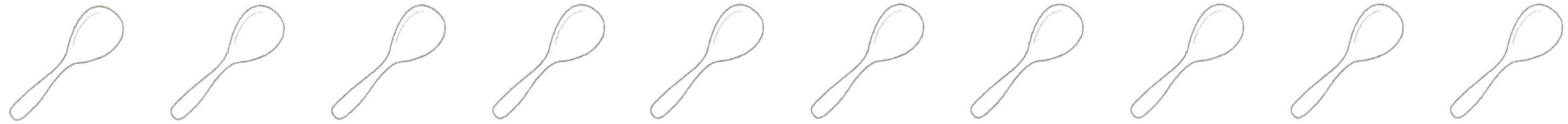

6

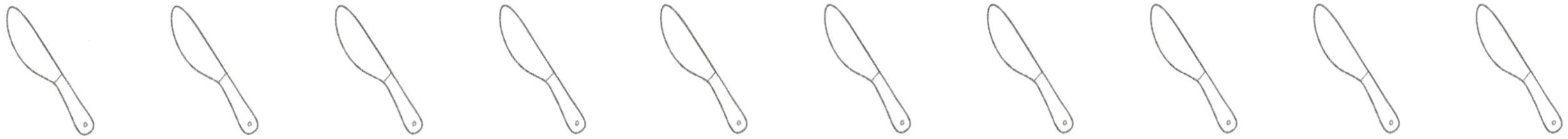

7

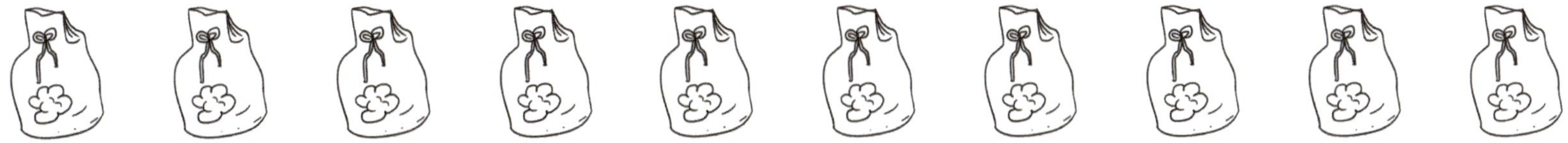

8

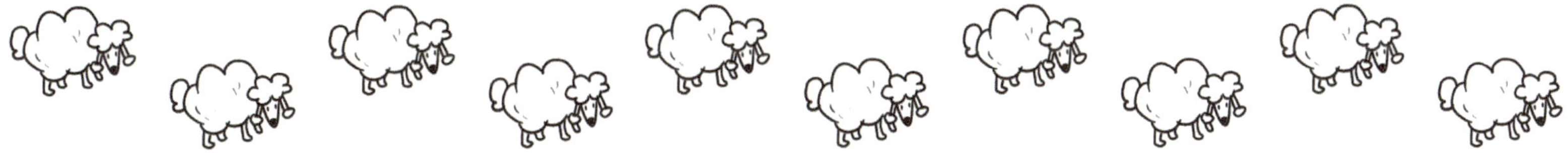

10

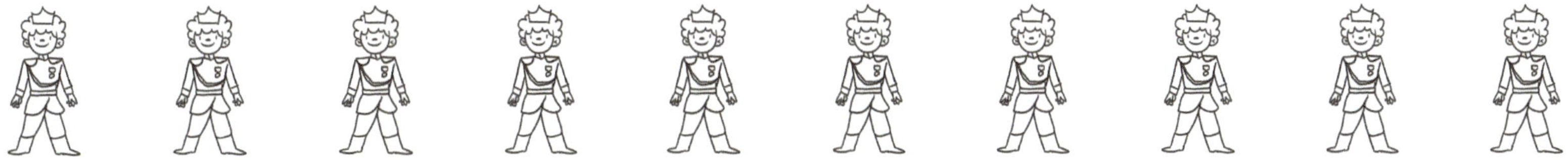

Masks

Masks

39

STORYLAND STORYLAND STORYLAND STORYLAND STORYLAND STORYLAND
STORYLAND STORYLAND STORYLAND STORYLAND STORYLAND
STORYLAND STORYLAND STORYLAND STORYLAND STORYLAND STORYLAND
STORYLAND STORYLAND STORYLAND STORYLAND STORYLAND
STORYLAND STORYLAND STORYLAND STORYLAND STORYLAND STORYLAND
STORYLAND STORYLAND STORYLAND STORYLAND STORYLAND
STORYLAND STORYLAND STORYLAND STORYLAND STORYLAND STORYLAND
STORYLAND STORYLAND STORYLAND STORYLAND STORYLAND
STORYLAND STORYLAND STORYLAND STORYLAND STORYLAND STORYLAND
STORYLAND STORYLAND STORYLAND STORYLAND STORYLAND
STORYLAND STORYLAND STORYLAND STORYLAND STORYLAND STORYLAND
STORYLAND STORYLAND STORYLAND STORYLAND STORYLAND
STORYLAND STORYLAND STORYLAND STORYLAND STORYLAND STORYLAND
STORYLAND STORYLAND STORYLAND STORYLAND STORYLAND
STORYLAND STORYLAND STORYLAND STORYLAND STORYLAND STORYLAND
STORYLAND STORYLAND STORYLAND STORYLAND STORYLAND
STORYLAND STORYLAND STORYLAND STORYLAND STORYLAND STORYLAND
STORYLAND STORYLAND STORYLAND STORYLAND STORYLAND
STORYLAND STORYLAND STORYLAND STORYLAND STORYLAND STORYLAND

Masks

Masks

43

ND STORYLAND STORYLAND STORYLAND STORYLAND STORYLAND STORYLAND ST
ORYLAND STORYLAND STORYLAND STORYLAND STORYLAND STORYLAND STORYLA
ND STORYLAND STORYLAND STORYLAND STORYLAND STORYLAND STORYLAND ST
ORYLAND STORYLAND STORYLAND STORYLAND STORYLAND STORYLAND STORYLA
ND STORYLAND STORYLAND STORYLAND STORYLAND STORYLAND STORYLAND ST
ORYLAND STORYLAND STORYLAND STORYLAND STORYLAND STORYLAND STORYLA
ND STORYLAND STORYLAND STORYLAND STORYLAND STORYLAND STORYLAND ST
ORYLAND STORYLAND STORYLAND STORYLAND STORYLAND STORYLAND STORYLA
ND STORYLAND STORYLAND STORYLAND STORYLAND STORYLAND STORYLAND ST
ORYLAND STORYLAND STORYLAND STORYLAND STORYLAND STORYLAND STORYLA
ND STORYLAND STORYLAND STORYLAND STORYLAND STORYLAND STORYLAND ST
ORYLAND STORYLAND STORYLAND STORYLAND STORYLAND STORYLAND STORYLA
ND STORYLAND STORYLAND STORYLAND STORYLAND STORYLAND STORYLAND ST
ORYLAND STORYLAND STORYLAND STORYLAND STORYLAND STORYLAND STORYLA
ND STORYLAND STORYLAND STORYLAND STORYLAND STORYLAND STORYLAND ST
ORYLAND STORYLAND STORYLAND STORYLAND STORYLAND STORYLAND STORYLA
ND STORYLAND STORYLAND STORYLAND STORYLAND STORYLAND STORYLAND ST
ORYLAND STORYLAND STORYLAND STORYLAND STORYLAND STORYLAND STORYLA
ND STORYLAND STORYLAND STORYLAND STORYLAND STORYLAND STORYLAND ST

Masks

45

Masks

47

Self-assessment Stickers